For You

FORGIVE THE BULLY
FOLLOW YOUR BLISS

Design by Austin Partridge
Edited by Cynthia MacDonald
Author Photo by Elaheh Mihar

Lightbulb courtesy of OpenClipArt.org

Published under the imprint Creative Culture

Library and Archives Canada Cataloguing
in Publication

Delorie, Oliver Luke, 1975-, author
        Dear Leroy : forgive the bully & follow your
bliss / Oliver Luke Delorie.

ISBN 978-0-9735918-5-9

1. Bullying--Juvenile literature. 2. Self-esteem--
Juvenile literature.
I. Title.

BF637.B85D45 2013   j302.34'3
C2013-907477-5

DearLeroy.com

TABLE OF CONTENTS

You are
sunshine.

DEAR LEROY

I nearly committed bullycide because I thought no one loved me. I actually believed what the bullies said.

They made me question what I looked like - my hair, my teeth, my clothes, my height, my weight, how I walked, how I talked, how I kicked a soccer ball, and how (in their opinion) unattractive to girls I was.

They made fun of my accent, my family, my house, my backpack, my drawings in art class, what I ate for lunch, where I sat, and my shoes.

It was hell and I thought it would never end.

I hope you are smarter than I am, and will do whatever it takes to stop getting pushed around and pressured by your friends to get into trouble, do drugs, drop out of school, or bully other kids.

Why listen to me? Because I was just like you.

I felt like sunshine, and bullies seemed like clouds that liked nothing more than to keep the sun off my face and my world cold and dark and gray, just how they seemed to like it.

But like me, you have something to share with the world, and it's up to you to find out what it is (and learn how to share it) so you can be free.

Fear is only
real if you
believe
in it.

FEAR

What do you do when you're scared?

Fear is a feeling that was programmed into us thousands of years ago when we had to hunt and fight saber-toothed tigers. It's not going to go away.

That means if fear is only a feeling (like sadness or happiness) it will always come and go.

If you are ever feeling scared, it's okay to fight, freeze or run away, but your feeling is not the enemy.

Don't be angry with yourself. Try not to be mean to your precious little self.

Most people fear fear. They are scared of feeling scared.

The sad thing is, this feeling stops them from doing the things they love to do. A feeling!

People are afraid of looking stupid, but who cares? You can always make fun of fear by laughing at it (doing this can turn bullies turn buddies, fyi).

If you are scared of someone or something, they are sucking your power away like a vampire.

Remember: vampires don't like the sun.

Getting bullied
is a good sign.
It means you
are different.

HATERS

What do you hate?

Hate poisons your heart.

It will quickly kill you, your friends, your family and your dreams before you even know what happened.

But only if you let it.

I want you grow up and be successful and happy. Isn't that what you want?

Hating the people who seem to hate you will only make you weak and sick, even if you are healthy.

When people hate someone or something, they are really hating themselves, but blaming everyone else for how awful they feel.

It doesn't make sense, does it?

I don't believe it's possible for anyone to really hate you. They don't even know you. They may think they do, but they don't.

Hating people will only make you lonely in the end.

Most importantly, the sun doesn't hate anyone.

How will you get the poison out?

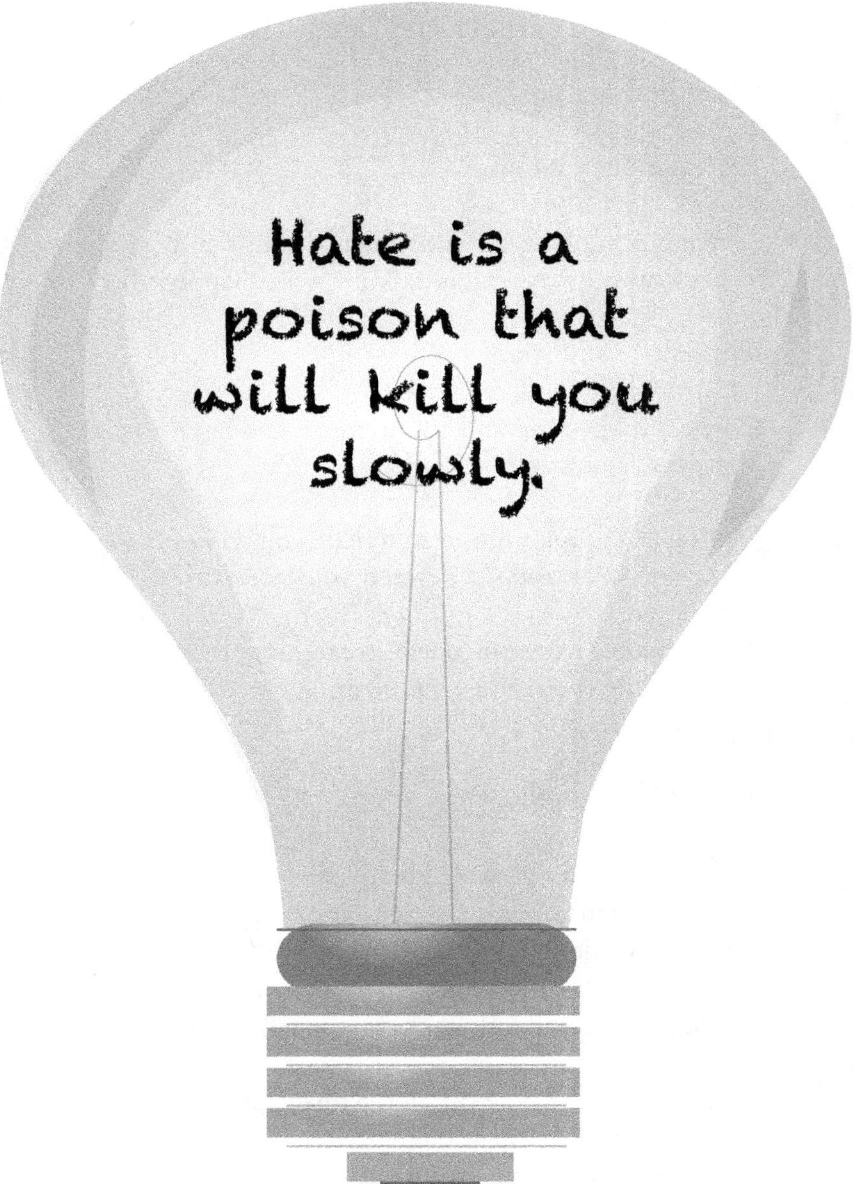
Hate is a poison that will kill you slowly.

FORGIVENESS

Has anyone ever asked you to forgive them?

What did you do or say?

The only reason bullies aren't buddies is because they don't like how much alike you are.

They would never admit this, of course.

I know it seems crazy, but I think it's true. Years after I graduated, a guy who used to bully me invited me over to his house to play music with him!

I have also dreamed of bullies asking ME for forgiveness. I almost couldn't believe it.

I know they didn't mean to hurt me, and I know they don't mean to hurt you. They are getting rained on by other clouds. It's not their fault. Remember that.

Of course, you are not a saint. You hurt people. You say and do things you wish you hadn't said or done. We all do. We are all clouds once-in-a-while.

The secret is to know it. Then do something about it.

But don't beat yourself (or the bullies) up because it's hard for you (and them) to change. Be patient and watch what happens when you forgive someone who hurt you.

Without confidence you won't be successful or happy.

ONE IN 7 BILLION

There is no one in the universe quite like you.

What makes you unique?

Just because you aren't good at something, doesn't mean you aren't good at something else.

There are billions of ways to do everything; as long as you aren't harming anyone, you are free to live your life however you want.

You are probably good at something, and could probably do it all day, every day, right?

Don't let anyone discourage you from turning your creative ideas or plans or projects into something you are proud of. You have to listen to your own inner voice.

If you're good at sports, play sports. If you like music, play music. If you're good at math... do math!

If you ever get lost in life and don't know what to do, remember what you like, and do that.

No one knows what you like as much as you do.

And please let other people do things the way they want. If you don't want to be criticized, don't criticize other people.

Forgiveness will heal all wounds.

FAILURE

Fear and failure are best friends. They hang out together, just waiting to rain on (and ruin) your life.

Unless you know what failure is, you will always be scared to try new things. Don't let your fear stop you!

What's the worst that can happen? You learn what didn't work. You thought something was one way and it turned out another way. You were wrong. Big deal.

You might be scared that your friends will laugh at you, but by the end of this book you will know a thing or two.

We all make mistakes, but most people give up and stop following their dreams. The only way you will fail is if you give up.

You have to keep shining, or the world will get cold and dark and lonely and that would suck.

The happiest, healthiest and wealthiest people in the world have failed more than anyone else. The founder of KFC heard "no" 109 times before someone tried his chicken recipe. Would you have given up after 1 "no"?

The more you fail, the faster you will get where you want to go. So, what are you going do the next time things don't go your way?

Do unto
yourself as
you would do
unto others.

ZOMBIES

You might have noticed zombies are loose at your school and they are drooling for a bite of your brain.

Watch out! All they need to do is take a bite and now you're a zombie too. Run!

Zombies are so busy looking for their next bite of brain that they don't seem to care about anyone or anything but themselves.

How do I know so much about zombies?

Because I used to be one. I even worked at a pizza place called Zombie's Pizza. I'm not kidding.

I was a dark cloud of despair, undead and loving it. I was on the road to nowhere and didn't care.

All I did was eat and drink and sleep-walk my way through work and school. And all my friends were zombies too, so I didn't even notice.

What if brains taste good to you? What then?

Stumbling around in dirty rags without regular showers and proper nutrition will get boring, trust me. No one wants to kiss a zombie.

So if you haven't been bitten yet, don't be!

Every second
you spend
making your
dreams come
true is
worth
it.

HAPPINESS

There is a reason bullies are not happy.

They don't spend their time doing what they like, or with people who make them feel good.

The problem is: *they think they do.* They think their tribe of gang members are their friends, but they aren't.

Their fellow lost sheep are lost too, in search of anything to ease the pain they don't know they feel.

Does that make sense?

Sometimes bullies grow up to be adults and STILL don't know what makes them happy. Can you believe that?

The problem is: they get jealous of anyone who listens to their inner voice and follows their heart. They don't like seeing something being done that they fear they can't do themselves (even though they could).

I wish they knew this, but they don't (which is why they rain on your parade). But you know what makes you happy, right?

If you don't know the answer, find out - and do it quick - because love, friends, happiness and fun are all waiting to follow you wherever you go.

Patterns repeat themselves. Patterns repeat themselves.

PATTERNS

Even though you shine like the sun, you are human and will do the same things over and over again.

What patterns are you repeating?

The happiest people on earth see everything as a learning opportunity. They don't let setbacks stop them, so why should you?

When you think of all the people and experiences in your life, imagine you are looking into a mirror and everything you see is a reflection of what you believe deep down inside.

As long as you think / feel / act as if your life is a certain way, you will always see evidence that proves these same thoughts / feelings / actions are true.

If you ever want to change your friends, your marks, your job, or your relationships, look for patterns and see if you can notice when you're about to make the very same choice for the 10th (or 100th) time.

You learned your patterns from your mom and dad, who learned *their* patterns from *their* mom and dad.

Ask yourself "why did I do that again?". It will either 1) drive you insane, or 2) make you smarter.

Choose wisely.

There is no
rush. Life is
not a race.

OPPOSITES

There are two sides to every coin (and two sides to every story) as you probably know by now.

Where it gets messy is when its not clear which side is which, and whose side is whose.

This doesn't mean that opposites aren't there (they are); they just love the game hide-and-seek just like everyone else.

So how do you see them if they aren't always obvious?

You take a guess.

Maybe you're right and maybe you're wrong, but at least you might see what a bully or frenemy wants or needs deep down inside behind their tough exterior.

Bullies only hurt you because they have been hurt too (but don't try to tell them this; people usually don't like to hear the truth about opposites).

We all act in opposite ways all the time. We think one thing, but do the opposite. We say one thing, but do the opposite. We want one thing, but end up chasing after the opposite for some silly reason.

The trick is to know that opposites exist. It will help you understand why we all do the things we do.

Find adults you trust and ask for their help.

RESPECT

Who do you respect? Who do you admire?

If you have been hurt, ignored, laughed at, teased, kicked, punched, spat on, humiliated, hated and/or disrespected, it's hard to respect people because you start to believe you're not worthy of their respect.

Can you see how things can turn sour and make your lips pucker faster than you can say fish-face?

It's kind of like doing the opposite of what we want, but then repeating the pattern. Crazy!

My favorite author likes to remind me that the sun never says to the earth "you owe me."

How could being unconditionally loving, patient and respectful - like the sun - change the world?

I hope you can see through the thin disguise of haters, loners and blood-suckers, because just like you, they want love and respect too.

Show these evil forces the love and respect they crave deep down and your life will be much easier.

Very few people do this, by the way.

Why not be one of them and be kind, considerate and generous with your attention?

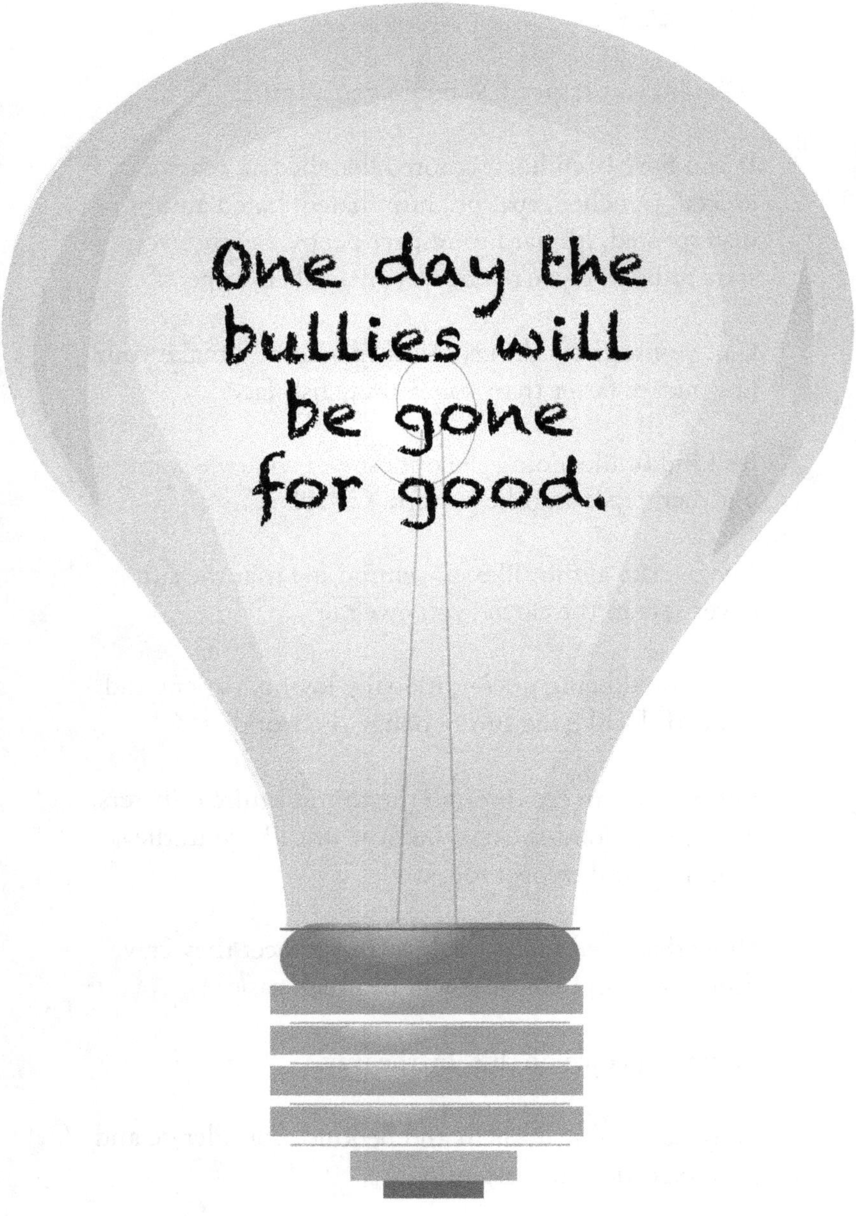
One day the
bullies will
be gone
for good.

CREATIVITY

Creativity is the greatest power in the world - just like the sun.

When you connect with the source of life, guess what?

Shazam! You can do anything you focus on.

Expressing your thoughts and feelings in whatever way you like will turn bullies into dust like the sun does to vampires, banishing them forever.

I see it happen over and over again.

Somehow, your unique creative force is like mosquito repellent that makes you smell like garlic to vampires and ensures you are undetectable to zombies.

Ever wanted your own invisibility cloak?

The secret to getting rid of bullies is simple: felt pens or paint or metal or wood or glass or software or tools or musical instruments or paper or fabric or food or film or chemistry sets or pixels. Just start playing and experimenting!

You are a genius, because no one will say it or draw it or sing it or build it or think it or design it or sew it or bake it or code it just like you.

How will you express what is bubbling up inside you?

Good and bad
come and go.
They always
have and
always will.

START A BUSINESS

People get paid to make and test video games, design software, help or heal people and/or animals, design and build buildings, grow food, take us into space, and solve myriads of pressing problems.

Some people like to connect people with products and services that improve their lives. Others make beautiful things with their hands, or outrun everyone on their team. Maybe you see solutions to problems not even your teacher can!

If you want to change the world, be your own boss! Start your own business, organization or charity.

Why wait until you're older? Do it now! Lots of kids do. Google it.

If your parents won't / don't / can't help, talk to your favorite aunt and uncle; your grandparents, or a teacher you like.

You will end up working twice as hard as everyone else, but 1) It's not work when you love it, 2) You will get to live your life how you want, and 3) There are no limits to what you can create out of thin air.

Remember: the cream rises to the top!

What will you create / build / sell / do / share / give?

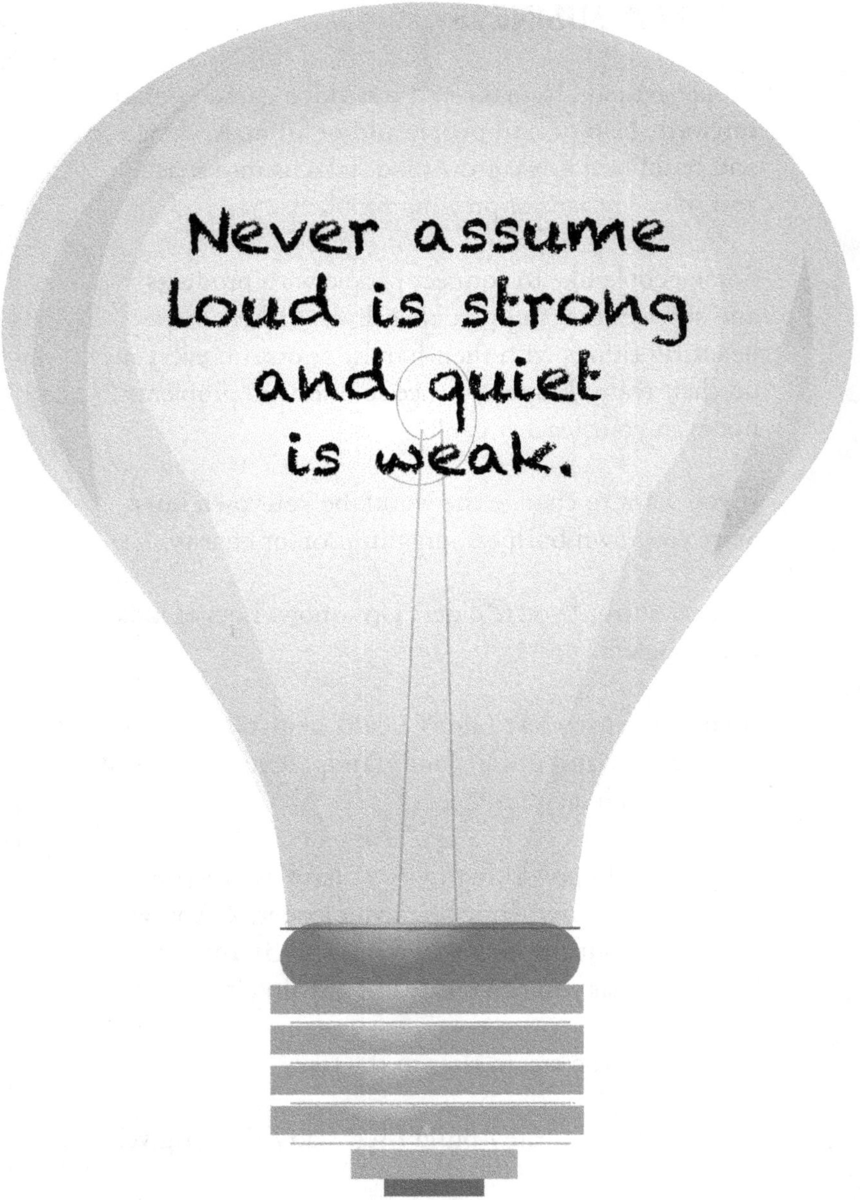
Never assume
loud is strong
and quiet
is weak.

VOLUNTEER

A wonderful way to learn new things and meet other people with similar interests is to volunteer an hour a week at an organization or charity or church or club that interests you and is doing work you believe in.

You're looking for your tribe. Give away your time and you will be welcomed into a new family.

Not only will you learn new skills for free, but you may also kickstart a new friendship, hobby or business (which will get you where you want to go even faster).

Sharing your time, money and/or energy with others will make you feel better than you ever have before.

You will smile more, your heart will beat slower, you will worry less, and you may fall in love.

The more you give, the more you get, but as you will see, it's not always from where you expect!

Contrary to popular belief, racing through life chasing fame and fortune will leave you feeling empty, unsatisfied and alone. What good is time, money and energy if you can't share it with other people?

Remember: does the sun ever say "no" to the earth?

Keeping all your wonderful gifts and talents and ideas to yourself is not only selfish, it's depressing. Boo!

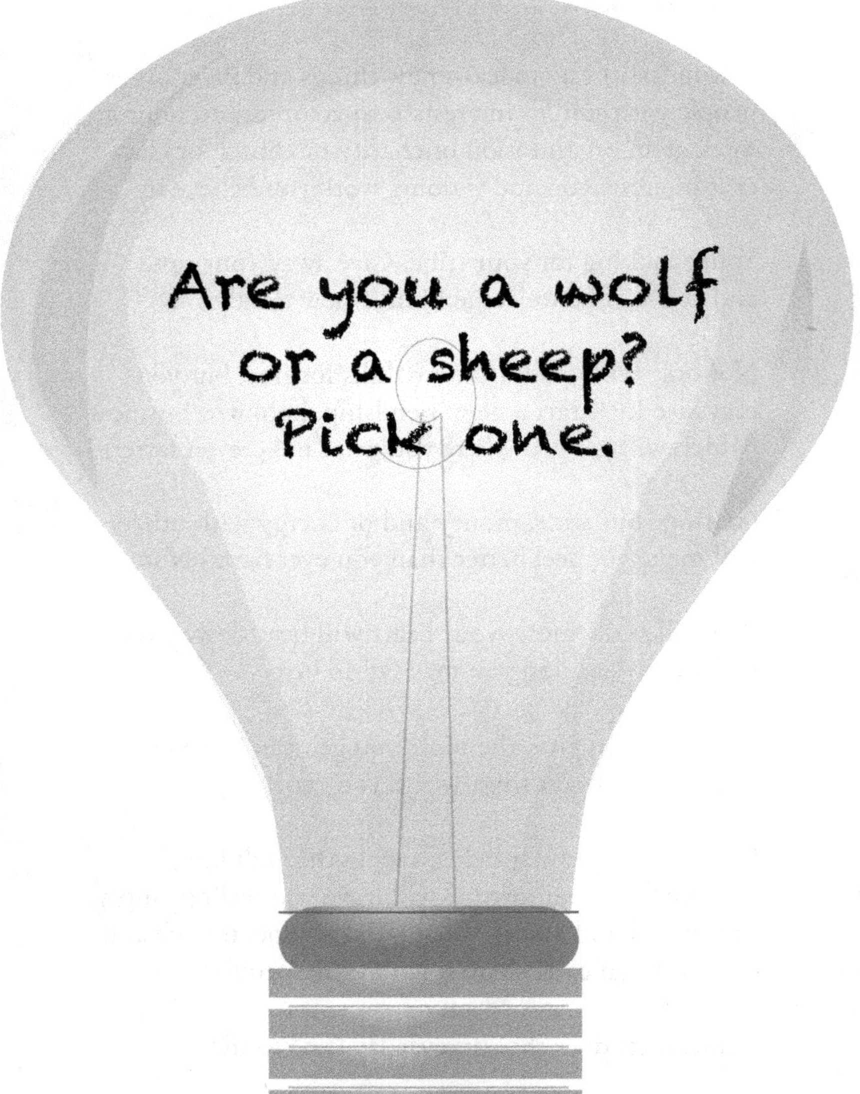
Are you a wolf
or a sheep?
Pick one.

DRUGS

Did you know people use drugs to escape reality because they don't know how to deal with their feelings?

When it's metaphorically cloudy all the time, it's easy for people to get depressed and look for happiness by putting toxic substances into their bodies.

They are usually scared or hurt or alone and don't know how to express themselves.

But you can express yourself! You know how. And you know that feelings of fear and failure aren't real (and you know how patterns and opposites work).

Drugs may seem harmless at first, but they will suck the love and respect you want into a blackhole, and turn your dreams into nightmares.

Drugs are one reason zombies are dead inside and out.

What do you know about the long-term side effects?

I used to do drugs because I thought it made me cool, but I wasn't cool. I thought I was invincible, but eventually doing drugs made me want to run away from everything (and everyone) I loved.

You need all the brain cells you can get, so hang on to them. You will want them later, I promise.

Zombies have very special needs.

ALCOHOL

Alcohol causes more problems in the world than you can imagine, which is why I'm asking you to wait until you are legally allowed to try it, if you want to.

Your brain and body are still growing and the last thing you want is to stunt your growth!

Did you know if you bend a tree when it is young, it will grow up crooked and bent?

Life is too full of opportunities and adventure to handicap yourself with a self-inflicted learning disability or put yourself in unneccesary danger.

You have enough problems to deal with growing up, and drinking alcohol will not only make your problems worse, it will give you more problems!

There is a legal drinking age for a reason. At least wait until you are an adult to start killing your brain cells.

Think of my 5D's if someone ever offers you alcohol.

Alcohol can...

- **d**epress you
- **d**ehydrate you
- **d**ull your senses
- **d**istract you from doing things you like
- **d**eplete your bank account

Define
happiness
for yourself,
because no one
knows it like
you do.

STRESS

Who or what stresses you out?

There are no right or wrong ways to do anything (as long as you aren't harming anyone or anything) so there are no right or wrong ways to get rid of stress.

If this means running until you can't run anymore, run. If this means dancing until you can't dance anymore, dance. If this means coding until you can't code anymore, code. You get the picture.

When I'm frazzled, I put on my apron and bake something or play drums or go for a walk.

What are 3 ways you can make stress disappear?

You may notice that the more responsibilities and relationships you have in your life, the greater amount of time, money, energy, attention and resources are required to make everything run smoothly.

But it's all worth it, because the more fires I put out, the greater the rewards... after the smoke clears, of course!

The solution is always simple: find something you love so much that you would do it for free.

Then everything else that seemed to matter so much won't bug you anymore (including bullies).

Want to
know what's
working and
what isn't?
Look in the
mirror of
your life.

GO FOR IT

Your life is going to seem short and it's going to seem long. Some days you will feel like you will live forever, while other days you will feel like you're almost dust.

Even the sun is going to burn out in billions of years, so hopefully that puts things in perspective: you don't need anyone's permission to do what you love.

Even if it seems like your parents or friends have it all figured out, they don't. No one does. All we all do is guess our best guesses, do what needs to be done, and (hopefully) do our best. That's it.

This is why you're free to blaze a new trail, take a short cut, see where that goes, and get back on track over and over again... as long as you live.

Enjoy the ride, because one day you don't want to wonder: why didn't I just GO FOR IT and now it's too late.

My favorite author also says: "don't die with your music still inside you."

Only you can sing the 'song' inside you. What 'song' will you sing?

When (not if) people judge or criticize your 'song' or say you can't 'sing' - just notice how it feels to prove them wrong. It's the best feeling in the world.

Put your life
in good hands.
Your own.

CRAZY LITTLE ANIMALS

Everyone is trying so hard to be 'normal' and civilized and well-behaved, but the more you try and be something other than yourself, the more your opposite will come out.

It's nothing to be ashamed of, but trying to hide it just makes it worse. It's like trying to hold a beachball underwater.

Let me explain:

1. We're "crazy" because we forget that opposites exist.

2. We're "little" because our inner child is pulling our strings and making us think or feel or do or say one thing, even when we think we want the opposite.

3. We're "animals" because humans lived in caves hunting and grunting for thousands of years longer than we've lived in boxes, texted, and gone shopping at the mall.

When things don't make sense, remember that you're a crazy little animal - just like everyone else.

It will help.

Just keep this fun little morsel of wisdom to yourself, because people often don't like what they don't understand (which is why bullies exist).

So what if your
life is back
to front and
upside down?

10,000 HOURS

I heard it takes about 10,000 hours (around 10 years) to get really good at something.

The more you practice something you like, the easier it will get, and the more fun you'll have doing it.

You've probably noticed how much better you are at a hobby or sport than when you first started.

If you keep at it, one day you'll be a master. Just think of all the possibilities!

So why not squish time?

Instead of spending 10 years to reach 10,000 hours, why not squeeze these 10,000 hours into just 5 years?

Wouldn't that be cool?

When you become a ninja or jedi knight, your favorite skill / hobby / sport / talent will become second nature, and your wish will become the world's command.

Why?

Because that's how it works. I've seen it happen over and over and over again.

But don't take my word for it. See for yourself.

There is only
one way to find
out if what you
believe is
true.

THERE ARE NO RULES

Whose and what rules do you live by?

I know you trust your mom and your dad, and your teachers and everyone else you're supposed to trust.

Following certain rules makes sense. Breaking some rules will only get you into trouble (as you may already know).

When I say there are no rules, I'm talking about the imaginary rules you make up about what's possible. As long as you are not hurting anyone, keep going!

If there's a voice in your head saying you can't do something, remember: you're a crazy little animal.

Who makes the rules by which you create something?

Don't let anyone (even your inner voice) trash-talk your dreams. Not even your best friend.

If they do, get rid of them and hang out with other sun-people who dig you.

People who make silly rules about what they (and you) can and can't do put limits on their unlimited lives.

Make up your own rules that give you the freedom to be yourself and try new things.

Just be safe, take care of people and have fun!

Learn from the pros how to do what you love to do.

MENTORS

Billions of people have explored every noun in existence. This is both good and bad news.

First the bad news: you have to flex your creative muscles a little harder than the zombies around you to come up with something original (which shouldn't be too hard, seeing as how you're so brilliant).

The good news: No matter what you like now (and what you become interested in when you're older) there are people who have done something similar.

Now the best part: they are everywhere, and your job (in addition to practicing your skill) is to find them.

The right one(s) will love helping you get where you want to go, and will be enthusiastic to talk about what has worked for them and what hasn't.

Working with a mentor who has been-there-done-that is the best way (again, in addition to honing your craft) to get where you want to go.

I hope you figure it out before I did. I thought I could do it all on my own, but that's impossible (and not to mention lonely, boring and expensive).

The most successful people in the world still have mentors and want to return the favor.

The only question is: what do you want to know?

2 steps forward
and 1 step back
will get you
where you
want to
go.

HIGH SCHOOL

While you are (stuck) in school, get a headstart on your business or mastering your favorite hobby.

Ask teachers you like for help. That's what the good ones are there for!

High school is basic education. Unless you are super-motivated AND talented AND have a mentor to help pave the way, seriously consider going to college.

No matter what, read books and blogs and figure out how to go to every conference or convention you can.

Spend time away from home and stay away long enough to see things (especially yourself) differently.

When you graduate, remember that student loans are a good investment. Cars aren't. Books are a good investment. Clothes aren't. Private lessons are a good investment. Beer isn't.

The more brain cells and creativity and skills you foster now, the more you will find what you are looking for when you grow up: love, friendship, good health, happiness and your version of success.

What will you do when you graduate?

Get the ball rolling now so you can make it happen when the day arrives.

Everything you see began with a single thought.

THOUGHTS ARE THINGS

If thoughts are things, would you agree that it makes
sense to make sense of things?

The fastest way to make sense of these thought-things
is by realizing that *how* you think of something
determines *how* the thing reacts.

What is true and what is not? What is true to you may
not be true to someone else - even your best friend.

Knowing this can help you maintain a level head
when the sun isn't shining and the sheep are (or aren't)
baaa-ing.

Instead of being fooled by the illusion that something
is as it seems, you know that every effect has a cause;
is connected; and is worth a closer look.

I like to say that reality is in the eye of the beholder.

Making an effort to understand the things in your
life that make sense (and the things that don't) is one
step towards becoming a leader, and doing what every
awesome person dreams of doing:

Kicking some ass doing what you love!

This is how successful people navigate their boats
to relative calm in the storms known as life, school,
work, family, relationships and love.

The secret to
success is to start
before you
are ready.

MINDFULNESS

One teacher says "mindfulness is paying attention, on purpose, in the present moment, without judgement."

Thinking only of the present moment while knowing that everything is temporary and nothing lasts.

Be mindful that less-than-desired grades are a sign (and opportunity) to improve, instead of giving up and going home.

Be mindful of making your own luck, so when opportunities arise, you can snatch them up and make it all seem easy.

Do you wait around for your friends and classmates to do or say things so you can relax?

If you can't chill, then no achievements / honors / scholarships / awards / prizes will have any effect.

You can practice mindfulness however you want.

You can close your eyes, take a deep breath, stretch, do yoga - all while simply focusing on the passing of time in a non-attached, non-judgemental way.

Concentrating on one thing at a time (versus multitasking) is a way to get into the creative state of *flow*.

Do this and everything else will fall into place.

You will always
do what is most
important
to you.

FOOD IS FUEL

If you are what you eat, are you a cookie? Kale salad? A soft-boiled egg? A stick of celery? A cheese burger?

Your friends and family probably have some influence over what you eat, when you eat, how you eat, and how much you eat.

If you are creative, artistic, open-minded or think differently than the oafs and ogres around you, you see doors where others see only walls; doors that lead places you could never have dreamed of.

But those doors will stay locked until you find the skeleton key that opens *every* door.

How do you get your hands on it?

Try eating colorful vegetables, drinking plenty of water, taking it easy on the junk food, eating small portions and actually chewing your food.

Health is happiness. Without it, nothing else matters (or is even possible).

Are you interested in being involved (at some stage) with what you put in your body?

Some people love to cook. Some people like to bake. Some people love to grow food. Some people just like to host dinner parties and eat with friends.

You will work
twice as hard
for yourself
but it won't
be work.

TIME

There seem to be few basic skills more valuable than mastering the management of your greatest resource.

My goal in this book is to arm you with a quiver of silver bullets to destroy the time-sucking monsters lurking in the shadows hungry to gobble up your most precious resource like they were feasting on the all-you-can-eat buffet you call life.

What would you do with another hour every day?

How would you spend an extra week every year?

It may seem like you're going to live forever, but you won't (you're not a vampire I hope).

So why not make the most of every day?

No matter how you choose to spend your seconds / minutes / hours / days / months / years, the truth is:

If it's important to you, you will make the time.

When someone says "I don't have time" what are they doing instead?

This will help you to know not only what your own priorities are, but also what other people cherish more than giving you (or someone or something else) the time it wants or needs.

It is
impossible
to give away
more than
you get.

WORRY

If the only thing to fear is fear itself, then the only thing to worry about is worry itself.

But why worry at all? If something is out of your control, there is nothing you can do about it. So why worry about it?

The past is history and the future is a mystery. There is only *now* and there will only ever be *now*.

Worry is a wish for what you don't want.

Worrying about other people, places or things does nothing to help said nouns.

In fact, some people believe that our thoughts have the power to affect those people, places and things (even if they are in far away places).

Instead of worrying about making a mistake, do what you want, get a result, and if it works, do it again. If not, trying something else until you get the result you want.

Do this repeatedly and worry will wither away. Don't lay awake tossing and turning all night dreading the future or regretting the past (which will tend to happen as you get older).

Worry isn't productive. Sleep is. Zzzzzzzzzzzzzzzzzzzz.

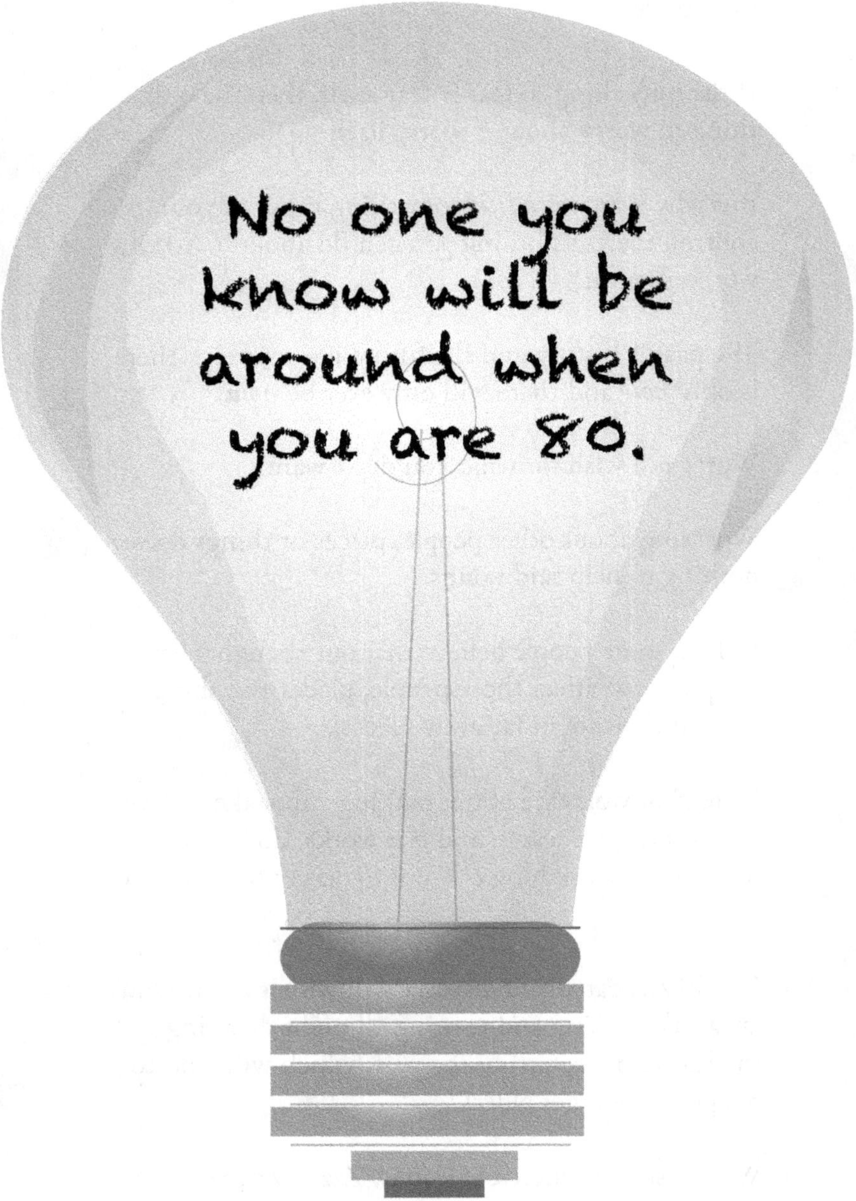
No one you
know will be
around when
you are 80.

PARENTS

Even when it seems your parents are on the war path; when they don't seem to get where you're coming from; when you consistently butt heads; when they get angry over what seems like nothing; or even when they punish you, remember: they still love you.

They always will.

Of course, if your parents *really* don't care - as in you don't feel safe - please ask someone you trust for help. Believe it or not, there are plenty of grown-ups who care.

Chances are your parents are likely responsible, supportive, kind folks who want nothing more than for you to be happy, healthy and successful.

No one gave your parents a manual on how to raise you. Be patient with them and give them a break.

Sometimes you seem like an alien to them!

The most significant adults in your life may have already joked with you about getting their revenge once you are a parent and have your own kids.

One day you will all be friends and laugh about it.

Developing a sense of humor (although dreadfully difficult at times) will make life easier. I promise.

The more brain
cells you have,
the more fun
you will
have.

FRIENDSHIPS

What do you like about your friends?

They probably like the same things you do: the same books; the same movies; the same food; the same clothes.

"Birds of a feather flock together" is a rhyme I like. That's what makes friendship so cool; sharing common interests, values, things you like and don't makes everything in life seem a whole lot easier.

But remember: just because you have a lot of friends, fans and followers online doesn't mean they are really your friends.

In a battle between quality versus quantity, quality always wins (unless you really don't care about people, but then you wouldn't have read this far).

Quality trumps quantity, because true friends are the best thing on earth!

Like the Irish proverb says:

There are good ships and wood ships
Ships that sail the sea
But the best ships are friendships
May they always be!

I love that, don't you?

Find ways to get naturally high instead.

SPIRITUALITY

The best advice I can give you about spirituality is this: believe what you want and enjoy life in your own way.

Yes, your parents wield a little influence; they will teach you (both consciously and unconsciously) what they believe, though when you start thinking for yourself, please know it's okay to make up your own mind if about stuff if you feel like you want to.

Some people say one thing is right and another is wrong. How can that be? Who made them judges?

If you don't believe me, take a look around. Opposing beliefs about life are the only reason people fight.

People fight because they believe their way is the only way, and they don't understand (and therefore don't like) people who make different choices.

It's ironic, because aren't 'good' people supposed to exemplify love, kindness, patience and compassion?

The problem may be religion itself, because I define 'spirituality' as our connection to the energy source that created all life and continues to make the grass grow with seemingly zero effort.

The point is this: you can listen to what other people say, or you can decide for yourself. It's up to you.

Question
anyone who
says that
something
is wrong.

EVERYTHING IS TEMPORARY

Your friends may not always be your friends and your family won't be around forever.

You will change jobs and live in different houses. You may even call different cities (or countries) home.

You may get married and you may get divorced.

Every relationship you ever have will blossom and grow and change and end in its own way, according to its own timetable.

It is pointless to try to control or hinder or block anyone or anything from making their own decisions or choosing what is right (or wrong) for them.

Throughout your life your heart will break (possibly many times). But your ability and capacity to love will also grow stronger and you will become more resilient.

The secret is to ensure the latter happens more than the former.

If everything is temporary, expecting the opposite in everything will allow you to go with the flow.

Remember this and you won't be so surprised and shocked when things inevitably transform.

Change is the only thing that doesn't change.

Work for
free and you
will see.

TRAVEL

Saint Augustine's mouth said "The world is a book.
Those who don't travel read only one page."

Wiser words of worldly wisdom for wondering
wanders have rarely been spoken.

Forget the 7 Wonders of the World; have you been to
another city? Another country? Across the ocean?

Most people are scared to leave their city, state,
province or country. But what they are most scared of
is facing the unknown.

They fear unfamiliar food, language, customs, clothes,
rules, ideas, trends, and getting lost or feeling lonely.

But no school, course, sport or hobby will give you
the same education as traveling (or living) in another
country (even for just a few months).

Do whatever you can to get away from home when
you graduate (even just for a summer).

Traveling alone (or with a friend) will change your life
I can't describe... well, because it's your life!

Wonders await you in distant lands that will blow
your mind (in a good way).

Are you up for adventure?

You are crazy,
but so is
everyone else.
Do whatever
you want
to do.

POPULARITY

Do you regularly step out of your comfort zone and take social risks (instead watching from the sidelines and waiting for someone else to make you rich, famous, popular, intelligent and successful)?

The secret ingredient in the recipe for popularity is:

Confidence!

How do you get confidence?

You give it to yourself by doing the things you like to do - instead of comparing yourself to everyone else.

Focus on what you love and the bullies will disappear.

Forget the drama at school and make something cool.

If you see an opportunity to participate in an event that seems awesome, dive in! Join a club or association focused on creating, promoting or celebrating ideas and projects that inspire you.

People focused on achieving their goals will be your best friends; these relationships will strengthen and deepen over time and bring you rewards for decades to come.

Making friends is easy when you speak from your heart (that's also how you find soulmates, btw).

Remembering where you came from will remind you of who you are.

MONEY

Just like zombies are addicted to brains, most adults are addicted to money. They think it will bring them love, happiness and respect (so they get hooked).

But money can't buy love; it can't buy happiness; and it doesn't buy respect. So if money can't give you the things you think you want, what's it good for?

Money makes it easier to exchange the value you create or provide for the goods and services you desire.

People get distracted chasing bigger and better stuff (and more of it) to help them ignore the fact they don't have the love, happiness or respect they want.

They must be hallucinating, because the best things in life aren't things; the best things in life are are free:

• Love
• Time
• Friends
• Family
• Laughing
• Inner Peace

It's ironic, but unless you can be happy with nothing, you will never be happy with anything.

Another way of saying this: if you can be happy with nothing, you will have everything.

The smartest,
friendliest
people are also
the coolest.
You'll see.

FINANCIAL FREEDOM

Consider yourself lucky.

Do these things and you will be better off than 90% of people in the world. That's a good start.

Why not retire long before anyone else (with more money to help you buy things you don't need, to please people you don't like).

If you earn money, put 10 cents of every dollar into your savings account and make an appointment to speak with a financial advisor.

Read blogs or go to the library and do some research so you can ask intelligent questions. Take notes!

Google "compound interest calculators" and see for yourself how much more money you will earn over your life by starting to invest now (versus waiting).

Saving and wisely investing your money is the best guarantee you have for (what I call) future financial freedom (3F), so you will be able to retire one day.

Investing your money will make you a dragon/vampire/zombie/you-name-the-monster-slayer.

P.S. If you want to be a millionaire one day, start now. Very few people do. You're welcome.

Take a risk.
The worst that
can happen is
you get a
different
result.

RADICAL ACCEPTANCE

Radical acceptance is difficult because few people accept themselves and their circumstances as they are.

If you can deal with your problems with the attitude that "this too shall pass" then you may just have found the answer to a long and happy life.

What are you going to do the next time you can't change something?

What will you say to all those mayhem-making monsters that will inevitably come marauding through your peaceful meadow or enchanted forest looking to do some serious damage?

Like fear and worry, the only other boobie trap you would do well to avoid is 'sweating the small stuff'.

If you can let nouns be nouns (resistance is futile) you may well enjoy another secret to life foreign to so many people.

What else are you going to do? Bang your head against a brick wall? Run away?

Vampires are not worth the blood loss; zombies are irrelevant, and princes(ses) will never be satisfied.

Same goes for people in the real world. Accept them as they are and move on.

Eat less or
exercise more
and your body
will thank
you.

EXERCISE

Sweating every day will help you find and follow your
bliss (and breathe the life into you that helps forgive
the big bad bullies). It's a fact.

If you love pizza, why not eat it once a week (instead
of every day) and burn it off dancing or shooting
hoops so you can live longer and eat even more pizza?

It's easy: walk or ride your bike instead of taking the
bus or driving. Go swimming or jogging or hiking.

Just as one of the simplests ways to take care of your
money is to either earn more than you spend, or spend
less than you earn, one of the simplest ways to take
care of your body is to either burn more calories than
you consume, or consume less calories than you burn.

If you are the type of person who could just crawl
into a jam-filled donut or sip soda from a fountatin at
Willy Wonka's all day (like me) earn it with exercise
(before or after you find solace in sweet sugar heaven).

If it's super hard for you to get off the couch or eat
your veggies, ask someone to help you get healthy.

Again, just taking the dog for a walk or dancing to
your favorite song with your earbuds in is a great way
to start losing weight and feeling great.

Because the healthier you are, the happier you will be.

Ask someone you admire for help. They will love it.

BABY STEPS

Hit songs, blockbuster movies, gold medals and lifetime achievement awards are impressive (and intimidating), although every rockstar, producer, athelete and actor started from scratch.

Some people have natural talent, wealthy parents, or an older brother or sister to look out for them, but so what if you don't?

The harder you have to work for something, the more it will mean to you. I mean it.

First, close your eyes and like Sponge Bob says "Use your imagination." Now think backwards and do some 'reverse engineering' and figure out - one step at a time - what needs to happen each step of the way.

Now take one step at a time until you get there.

You can always edit your book, draw another picture, go back to school, try out for the team next year, study harder for the next exam, or redo anything.

You can always correct what other people call mistakes, because if you love something, you will always get better at it. That's what successful people do.

Don't waste your time watching and judging others.

What does the first step toward your goal look like?

When it comes to expressing yourself there are no rules.

YOUR PURPOSE

What were you born to do?

No one knows the answer to this one better than you.

My mentor asked me: "If you had one chance to speak to 50,000 people, what would you say?"

It's all in this book! What would *you* say?

Nothing will squash the blood-suckers swarming around you better (or faster) than defining your mission in life and moving towards it every day.

Figuring out what you love to do more than anything (and then doing it) is the most important job you have. Don't wait for someone to give you permission.

Without passion for your personal mission, you may never get what you want out of life.

This is what leads people to commit suicide and do drugs and turn into brain-devouring cannibals (or even worse: stumble through life like the undead relying on everyone else for survival).

I don't know about you, but as romantic as being a vampire might be for the first few weeks, the fun quickly fades as soon as the novelty wears off.

What were you born to do?

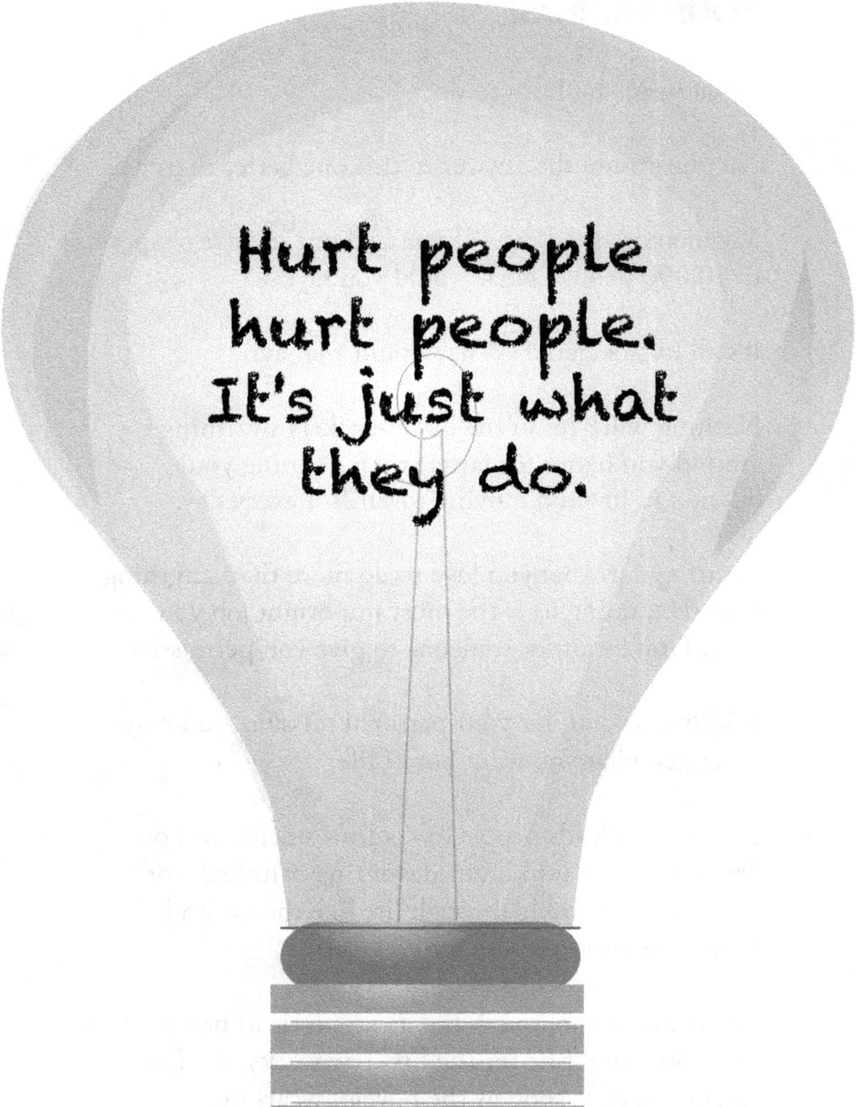
Hurt people
hurt people.
It's just what
they do.

ROTTEN APPLES

Unfortunately, some apples rot on the tree (if they even grow into fully-formed fruit at all).

They don't get enough water or sunlight or fertilizer. Or maybe the tree is old and tired.

Whatever the reason, even 'deformed' apples are a natural part of life. They exist, don't they?

I'm talking about people.

Maybe you know some rotten apples at school (maybe some adults you know seem extra crabby).

You may not like one of your teachers, but they aren't rotten apples; your relationship with them (a 2-way street, btw) is what's rotten. But that's another book.

You have 2 choices:

1. Be frustrated, angry and miserable about it.
2. Accept that rotten apples will always be falling from trees and attracting worms.

The first choice will turn *you* into a bully and make you no better than those you wish to banish.

The second is much easier. Juice (yum!) the rotten apples or leave them alone. You always have a choice.

The more you
learn the more
you earn.

COLLEGE

College is a blast!

It will seem like a whole other galaxy; high school will seem light years away.

College is a chance to start over, find your tribe, and have some fun (all while gaining invaluable skills in business, your favorite trade, or your chosen career).

Some of the friends you make at college will be your friends forever. Sweet!

You may meet the person of your dreams (it happens all the time) while exploring a variety of courses, activities and creative projects.

You can dip your toes into anything your heart desires and enjoy the support and resources of professors and institutions ready and willing to help you.

Student loans are one of the best investments you can make, for education is the biggest indicator of success, enabling you to earn more money over the course of your life (versus working at a minimum wage job).

Better careers, business ventures and creative pursuits pay off better than crappy, minimum-wage gigs every day of the week.

Remember: the more you learn, the more you earn.

Love is
like a butterfly.
Chase it and
it flies away.

LOVE

Love is like a butterfly. Chase it and it will fly away.

Follow your bliss and love will find you.

You will know it's true when he or she or they comes and finds you, for "time is to love what wind is to fire; it extinguishes the small and enkindles the great."

These marvelous morsels of wisdom have kept my heart warm whenever life has taken a left turn.

But you can't always control your heart. It will love who and when it wants. You may have no say in the matter!

Whether you have been in love or not; whether you've been on a date or not; whether you have a partner or not; and whether you have your eye on someone (or not) doesn't change the fact that you want to give and receive love.

Be patient. It will happen. Remember the butterfly.

And keep in mind that couples who stay together for 50 years go through ups and downs. There are no rules (except the ones you make up together).

What fun!

Enjoy the game of love like you enjoy the game of life.

You are
loved.

TRUST YOURSELF

I love the saying "The best way to predict the future is to create it."

As I have stated numerous times throughout this book (enough already!) you can reinvent yourself daily.

Can you tell what I'm passionate about?

I cannot emphasize enough that new surroundings (such as other countries and cultures) help a lot.

You can overcome most challenges as long as you don't give up. But if you think you can't do something, you're probably right.

If you want something, don't wait for other people to give you permission or say YES or OK or GO!

Too many people follow everyone else around like sheep, while vampires prey on their souls, suck the life out of them, and leave them cursed as they themselves are, shivering in the shadows cast by their dark clouds.

But not you. You shine like the sun!

And you are always shining, even when it feels like you could contentedly hide behind the clouds.

We need the sun, just like we need you.

Endless luck to you, bully-cloud-banisher!

WHY I WROTE THIS BOOK

Before I was born, my uncle Phil wrote me a letter and began it with *Dear Leroy...* My mum still won't give it to me.

Years later, after escaping (dropping out of) my third high school, my cousin lent me her acoustic guitar.

I slowly taught myself to play and began expressing myself with words and music, eventually learning how to write and record simple songs.

Within months, I had empowered myself with what I call *Creative Confidence,* because when I returned to a new school the following September I was bully-proof.

I didn't know it at the time, but it worked!

The most valuable lesson I learned on my journey from bloodless victim to vampire slayer was the courage to trust my creative process and take risks.

I like to say *I learned more than I thought there was to know* so I wrote this book to help you express your unique creativity, connect with the people you care about, and celebrate your life in your own unique way.

You too can *forgive the bully and follow your bliss.*

I wish you all the confidence and creativity in the world.

Oliver Luke Delorie
June 15th, 2018